Tips for Makeup
Simple and Detail Make Up Guides for Beginners

Copyright © 2021

DEDICATION

Contents

Introduction

The power of makeup is undeniable; our favorite products help us create the beauty looks we love, enhance our favorite features, and encapsulate our individual definitions of beauty. The best makeup routines help the modern woman boost her confidence and face the world head on—no matter what the day has in store.

When it comes to makeup, skillful application can make all the difference. Applying your favorite products the correct way can do two things: help you achieve the beauty look you crave, and help you get the most out of your makeup.

Learn how to apply your makeup with these important beauty tips. From applying liquid foundation to using a gel eyeliner, these tips and tricks will help you create a flawless look that you can be proud of.

50 Makeup Tips You Have To Know

Take a look at your makeup arsenal and think of all the masterpieces you can create with it. What if we tell you that your eyeshadow palette can be used for a lot more than just adding color to the eyelids? Or, let you in on some tricks that would make sure that your cat eyes and wings are on fleek every single time? It doesn't matter if you are a beginner or a pro at makeup, tips and hacks always come in handy. It is smart to get your money's worth by using the same product in multiple ways. Here are 50 makeup tips that will make sure you look your best at all times.

1. Make Sure Your Primer Complements Your Foundation.

Whether oil or water, your primer and foundation should share the same base; otherwise, they will repel each other or just slide off your face, making it difficult to blend.

2. Make Crow's Feet Disappear.

Dabbing a little amount of primer around your eyes dramatically minimizes the appearance of crow's feet.

3. Right Application For Right Coverage.

While putting your foundation on, if you want sheer coverage, use your fingers. But, if you want a full coverage, use a foundation brush.

4. Avoid Peach Fuzz.

Always apply foundation using downward strokes. Most of us have a thin layer of hair on our face, and applying foundation in an upward stroke will make the hair strands stand out. Looking fresh and pink like a peach may be your goal, but highlighting your peach fuzz definitely shouldn't be.

5. Create A Conical Shape.

Most of us are used to applying concealer in a semi-circular pattern under our eyes to reduce the appearance of the bags or puffiness. However, for best results, apply the concealer in a conical pattern under the eyes and extend it to almost where your nose ends. It not only does a better job at concealing because it is easy to blend, but it also helps in contouring the sides of your nose.

6. DIY Color Correcting Palette

You probably, by now, have heard about the wonder called color correcting palette. These concealers of various hues are used to cancel out flaws on your face. For example, a green concealer is used for canceling out any redness, lavender for yellow toned discolouration, peach for bruises or blue toned under eye circles, etc. But if you suddenly find yourself without your color correction palette or just want to save money, just mix an eyeshadow of the color you want your concealer to be with your normal concealer – and voila! You have your smart and cheap color corrector concealer palette.

7. Know The Important Focal Points.

This hack is for those days when you are running late or just feeling too lazy to apply your concealer properly. Just dab on a little concealer, preferably with a brush, under your eyes, on the corners of your mouth, and near your nose, and you are good to go.

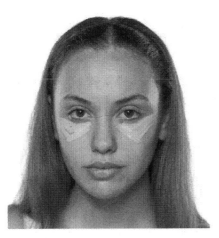

8. Know The Correct Function.

There are mainly two types of face powder – loose powder and pressed powder, and both come in dewy and matte finishes. It is important to know which one to use for what purpose. Loose powder is basically used to set the makeup in place and make it long-lasting. Though it comes in both tinted and translucent forms, it is best to use the colorless translucent one for setting the makeup as it will not disturb the color of your foundation and concealer. Pressed powder, however, is best suited for touch-ups on the go. Also, a dewy finish gives a glowing appearance to the skin, and a matte one provides a porcelain look with fine textures.

9. Choose The Right Brush.

The result of any makeup product largely depends on the applicator, and this is especially true for powders. Always use the fluffiest brush you can find to put your powder on for best results.

10. Blush Under Foundation.

This is also a clever way of reversing the order of applying the product to get smashing results. All you have to do is apply the blush first and then apply the foundation over it. The end result looks like you are glowing naturally from within.

11. Use A Tissue Paper For Blotting.

Instead of blotting your blush with a powder, use a tissue paper. Press it lightly over the blush after application and finish off with your makeup sponge or beauty blender for that perfect flush of color on your cheeks.

12. Be Careful With Shimmery Blushes.

It is tricky to pull off a shimmery blush perfectly. In fact, it is a good idea to skip shimmery blushes altogether if you have large pores, pimples or other symptoms of troubled skin.

13. Apply In A Triangular Fashion For Better Blending.

Though it's a common practice to apply bronzer with a fluffy brush on the hollow of your cheeks, it is a better idea to draw two inverted triangles on your cheeks with a bronzer. Blend it out, and you will have the perfectly done bronzer that will give you perfectly chiseled features.

14. DIY Bronzer.

If you are in the mood for trying out something fun, try making your own bronzer. All you need are a few items that are already sitting on your kitchen shelf. Take some cinnamon powder, cocoa powder, some nutmeg powder, and mix with some cornstarch – and there you have your bronzer. If you are a fan of makeup with natural ingredients or want to keep chemicals completely at bay, it doesn't get any more natural than this.

15. Feathery Strokes.

Always use light feathery strokes while filling out your eyebrows with a pencil. It will make them look more natural.

16. Instant Eye Lift.

For an instant lift in the eyes, use your highlighter just above the arch of your brows and blend it out. It will not only define your eyebrows perfectly but also have a dramatic impact on the appearance of your entire face.

17. Donning Many Hats.

This is one of the most versatile soldiers of your makeup arsenal. Eyeshadow can be used as a blush, bronzer, highlighter and even to slightly alter the color of your base makeup items.

18. Get The Pop.

If you are stuck with an eyeshadow with less pigment or you want that extra pop of color, create a white base by filling in your eyelids with a white eyeliner pencil first.

19. Proxy For Eyeliner.

On the days when another battle with your eyeliner seems impossible or you just want a soft look, take an angular brush and use eyeshadow instead of an eyeliner on your upper lash line. It gives a natural and breezy look, absolutely perfect for summers.

20. Dots And Dashes To The Rescue.

It might sound lame to a few, but there are people (like me) for whom drawing a straight line on paper is a task difficult enough, let alone exhibit such mastery on eyes with an eyeliner. Fret not, just draw small dots or dashes with your eyeliner on the lashline and join them. Perfectly done eyeliner in a jiffy.

21. Scotch Tape Method.

For a perfect wing, use the scotch tape method. Just stick a scotch tape in an angular fashion on the sides of your eyes and let the ends guide you to achieve that killer winged eyeliner every single time. You can also use a spoon, business card, debit card or basically anything with a straight edge as a guide.

23. Go Natural With Tightlining.

Try tightlining for the perfect no makeup look. Instead of putting the eyeliner on the lashline, apply it beneath the line. Make sure you use a waterproof variant for this one.

24. Use A Shadow To Lock It In.

Use an eyeshadow of the same shade as the eyeliner to set the liner in place.

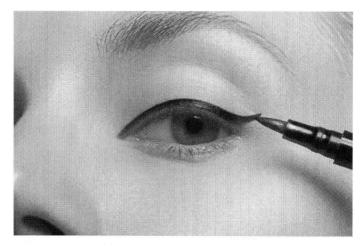

25. Prevention From Smudging.

When it comes to smudge prevention, kajal is not the easiest product to work with. However, to ensure your kajal stays put for hours, simply dab some eyeshadow over it once you are done. You can also use an eyeliner. Simply draw a line with the liner over your kajal. It will lock the kajal in place and also look super neat.

26. Hassle Free Smokey Eyes.

For a quick smokey eye, apply kohl on your upper and lower lashlines and waterline and then smudge it. Finish off by drawing a sideways 'V' on the outer corner and blend well. Rock the sultry smokey eyes for a night out.

27. Easy Removal Of Kajal

Removing kajal from your eyes can be quite a task. Simply dip a Q-tip into a cleansing lotion and carefully remove the kajal with it. Avoid poking yourself in the eyes.

28. Use Tissue Paper To Eliminate Clumping.

To prevent mascara from clumping, wipe off the excess product on a tissue paper before every application.

29. Use Baby Powder For Thicker Lashes.

If you want your eyelashes to plump up, follow this technique. First, apply a coat of mascara and then dust some baby powder on it. Then, apply a second coat. It will instantly give your lashes dramatic volume.

30. Contact Lens Solution Is The Solution.

Instead of scrapping your flaky mascara, add a few drops of the same solution you clean your contact lenses with to it. The formula would be back to a usable consistency. You can also put the tube in a glass of warm water to liquefy the formula.

31. Preserve Your Mascara Applicator.

Once you are done with a tube of mascara, do not throw away the applicator. You can use the applicator as a spoolie for your brows.

32. Start From The Middle.

For a defined cupid's bow, draw an 'X' where your cupid's brow should be, and then apply the lipstick normally. Even if you do not plan to highlight your cupid's bow, start applying the lipstick from the middle of your lips and move outwards for a flawless finish.

33. Practice Overlining With Caution.

If you want your lips to appear slightly bigger, you can consider overlining your lips, that is, putting your lipliner outside your lips. However, be careful while doing this. If you go overboard, it will look too obvious and exceptionally tacky. For best results, apply along the outer margins of your lips.

34. Make It Last Longer.

To make sure your pout looks perfect for the longest time, dab a little translucent powder onto your lips after you apply your lipstick. You can also use a colorless eyeshadow for the purpose. If you use a shimmery eyeshadow, it will also act as a highlighter and give your lips that extra dimension.

35. Apply The Lip Liner After Lipstick.

I know it sounds a little odd, but according to some experts, if you put lipstick first and then go for the lipliner, you will know exactly how to line. Also, when they start fading, they will fade together.

36. The Thumb Rule.

Getting lipstick on your teeth is surely not a look you were aiming for, but it happens more often than we care to admit. In order to avoid it, put your thumb inside your lips, pucker up, and pull the thumb out.

37. Know Your Brushes.

No matter how exclusive your products are, everything depends on the application. Thus, brushes are of extreme importance. Know which brush to use for what purpose. Yes, with a number of options at your disposal, remembering which brush does what can be daunting. Take time to figure all that out, and till then, remember that fluffy brushes are good for diffusing products like powder or blush, and small brushes are used for products that require precision, like eyeliner and lipstick.

38. Clean Your Brushes.

There is absolutely no excuse for not cleaning your brushes, unless a serious skin breakout is the look you are going for. Unclean brushes are breeding grounds for bacteria and makeup residues impact their performance as well. Clean them with a mild shampoo at least once a week.

39. DIY Fan Brush.

Brushes can be expensive, and the plethora of varieties can be daunting to choose from. So, if you have been eyeing that perfect fan brush but your pocket has been looking at the other side, don't lose heart. Simply take a bobby pin and fix it where the bristles of your blush brush start, and there you have your perfect fan brush to nail than contouring.

40. Wet The Tip Before Application.

To get the best out of your intense or shimmery shadows, gently spray your brush with a little makeup setting spray. If you do not have a setting spray handy, just dip the tip of the brush into water for the desired intense effect.

41. Follow The Correct Order.

It is important to follow the right order of applying makeup to ensure you get the best finish. Though it is a common practice to start base makeup first, beauty experts suggest that you start with your eyes and brows. In fact, it is also a good idea to do your foundation, concealer, and powder in the end, so that you can easily cover up all the mistakes for an end result that is flawless.

42. Do Your Makeup Under Natural Light.

Try to do your makeup in as much natural light as possible. Makeup looks different under different artificial lights. It is only in natural light that you can understand the real deal.

43. Cool, Warm or Neutral?

Know your color tone. There are basically three tones – warm, cool and neutral, and it is important to know yours to find makeup products that have undertones to suit your color tone. An easy way to tell which tone you are is to check the color of your veins. If you have bluish or purplish veins, you have a cool tone. If they appear green, you have a warm tone, and if you have trouble telling, you are probably of a neutral tone.

44. Walk Into The Mist.

Your makeup is usually incomplete without a dash of your favorite perfume. However, don't empty the bottle on yourself. If it's a strong fragrance, instead of directly spraying it, spray it above your head, a little away from your body, and walk into the mist. It will distribute the fragrance evenly and linger on.

45. Make Your Own Palette.

Whether it a concealer palette or an eyeshadow palette, there are always only a few colors that we use. Palettes are usually expensive, so buy refill eyeshadows of the colors you like and set them in an empty box to make your own palette comprising of products you will actually use. It can save you a lot of money as single colors or refills cost way less than palettes.

46. Heat Your Eyelash Curler.

Blow your hair dryer on the eyelash curler before curling your lashes. The heat will help you to get perfectly curled lashes instantly. However, make sure the dryer is on low heat mode and test the temperature on your hand to avoid getting burned.

47. Use Waterproof Products Carefully.

Although water resistant products are good for long wear and stay put, extended exposure to such products can cause harm to your skin. As water resistant products require a lot of rubbing or special products to remove, wear and tear of the protective layer of the skin is highly possible.

48. Rubbing Alcohol Miracle.

The next time your compact, blush or eyeshadow breaks, don't worry. Just add some rubbing alcohol and hold it in place. Let the alcohol evaporate and say hi to your restored cosmetics.

49. DIY BB Cream.

Mix your own primer, foundation, sunscreen, and compact powder to make your DIY customized BB cream.

50. Sharing Is Not Caring.

It is not hygienic to share makeup items, even with your closest friends. There is a huge chance of infection spreading. Especially refrain from sharing eye and lip products.

The world of makeup is huge and full of wonders. Explore the world and keep discovering new ideas to express yourself through makeup. Hoping these 50 makeup tips will help you to look at the multitude of possibilities and keep the makeup adventure junkie in you alive.

Also, let us know your feedback in the comments section below.

Expert's Answers for Readers Questions

Does wearing makeup damage your skin?

No, makeup normally doesn't have any major negative effects on the skin, but it depends on the skin of the person. There can be different types of skin reactions due to a common ingredient present in the products. These reactions are most commonly caused by things like fragrances or preservatives present in the makeup products. Following a proper skin care regime every day will help prevent skin damage.

Does makeup cause wrinkles?

The makeup and the environmental pollutants that get accumulated on your skin through the entire day slowly seep into your pores and break the collagen and elastin. This speeds up the aging process and can cause fine lines and wrinkles.

This is the reason it is very important to cleanse and moisturize your skin every night before going to bed.

Does makeup make you look older?

No, it doesn't. In fact, wearing the right products for your skin and using the right techniques to apply makeup will make you look younger and fresher. Less is always more, so use less makeup and wear shades like pinks and corals on the eyes and cheeks to look more youthful.

Does mineral makeup help acne?

Yes, mineral makeup is considered as the best product to use if you have acne as it contains only natural minerals. Also, the benefits it provides are numerous. Mineral makeup does not contain oils, fragrance, and preservatives that cause irritation and aggravate acne. Most of the mineral-based products are non-comedogenic, which means they don't clog your pores.

5 Pro Tips That Help Your Makeup Last Longer

1. BLOT BEFORE YOU APPLY PRIMER

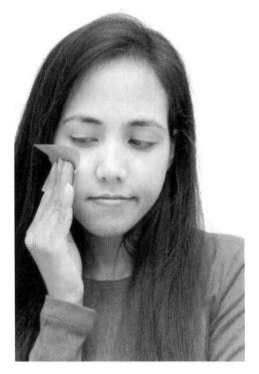

The skincare products that you apply before your makeup routine such as serums and moisturisers may contain oil. While most of them should be absorbed by your skin, there may be some excess oil that remains on the surface of your skin.

This is why you should use a blotting paper to gently dab your entire face before you apply the primer and begin your makeup process. This ensures makeup goes onto a more matte surface and is able to stay on for a longer time. Take note not to be over-zealous with the dabbing and dry out your face instead. The idea is simply to get rid of the excess grease.

2. BUILD UP FOUNDATION SLOWLY

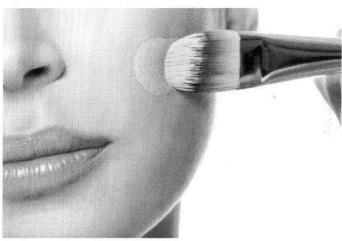

Do you have the habit of dispensing an entire pump of foundation and applying everything onto your face? This may be convenient but could mean you're applying too much foundation – which can mean more budging later.

Instead, pump out a small amount first and focus on just one section of your face. Slowly pat out the foundation to achieve the thinnest layer possible with the level of coverage that you require. Then, pump out more and repeat the same at another section.

If you're not worried about product wastage, and value convenience, you can dispense a full pump onto the back of your hand and slowly build up your foundation as described above. You can wash away any foundation that you didn't use.

3. SWEEP ON SOME POWDER BEFORE DOING YOUR BROWS

If you're one of those who notice their brow makeup coming off quickly, this is the trick for you. After your foundation, sweep on a thin layer of powder first before applying brow makeup.

The sequence of brow makeup application is also important. Always start with products with creamier texture and end with those in powder format. In other words, if you typically use a pomade and and brow powder, the pomade so go before the powder.

4. PRIME YOUR EYELIDS

Our eyelids get oily after a while, this is why it's important to prime them before applying eyeshadow. Besides using an eyeshadow primer before you apply the colours, you can consider sweeping some translucent powder after you're done too. Another great trick to try: apply cream eyeshadow to achieve the intensity that you want, then tap on some powder eyeshadow in the same shade to seal it in further.

5. LAYER YOUR BLUSH

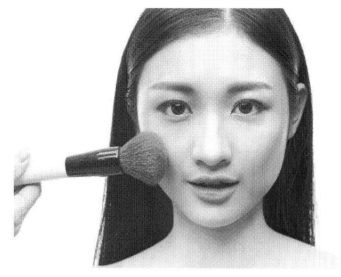

Amateurs apply blusher in one minute. But if you watch the pros at work, you'd notice they tend to spend more time. This is because many experts layer on their blush. Here's a recommendation to try: apply cream blush first, then layer on powder blush in the same shade. Alternatively, consider using a cream blush first and then powder highlighter on top of it. This way, your glow will last a lot longer than before!

Steps To Applying Makeup

STEP 1: MOISTURIZER

Before you begin applying your makeup, take the time to prep your skin with a high-quality moisturizer. Choosing the right kind of moisturizer is a crucial piece of the puzzle. Let's take a look at the different types you can use, listed from lightest to heaviest:

Face Mists: These are water-based solutions that may contain certain skin-boosting vitamins and fragrances. Facial mists aren't designed to return the moisture to your skin, but they can be a helpful tool for maintaining a dewy look all day long. Simply spritz throughout the day when your skin is feeling dry.

Serums: This is a lightweight solution that's easily absorbed by the skin. There are a wide assortment of serums designed to target specific problem areas. Some serums help you moisturize the skin to prevent wrinkles, while others contain ingredients that may add brightness to a dull complexion.

Lotions: Lotions are the most common type of moisturizer, and can benefit a variety of skin types. Opt for lotions that are labeled as "non-comedogenic"; these products are designed to avoid clogging the pores.

Creams: If your dry skin needs extra help, it might be time to invest in a cream moisturizer. This is a thicker, heavier solution that can hydrate excessively dry complexions. Day creams can be used as a base under your makeup, but night creams are designed to give your skin an extra dose of moisture while you sleep. Apply before hitting the pillow, and in the morning you'll be greeted with soft, supple skin.

Oils: If you need further moisturizing, consider oils. Certain oils can be a great option for those with dry, sensitive, or normal skin. However, if you're acne-prone or struggle with oily skin, avoid oil moisturizing products.

Learning how to apply moisturizer correctly is half the battle. Pour a small amount onto your fingers—the dollop should be roughly the size of a quarter. Start by spreading the moisturizer across your forehead; begin from the center of your face, then move outwards and up. Then, do the same starting at your nose, spreading the moisturizer across your cheeks. Ensure you've rubbed in the moisturizer evenly across your skin to avoid clogging your pores. Once you've applied enough moisturizer, gently rub it in using circles, and give it a few minutes to dry before moving onto the next step.

STEP 2: PRIMER

Now that your skin is well moisturized, prep your face with primer. Whether you're planning on applying a light coat of foundation or a full face of makeup, primer is an important first step. Using primer under your makeup will make your look last longer.

So what exactly is primer? Think of primer as a base for your foundation or face makeup that will help it go on smoother and last longer. Primers are silky smooth gels and creams that fill in the lines and pores on your face, smoothing out uneven textures and creating the ideal canvas for your makeup.

To apply your primer, begin by squeezing a small amount onto your fingertips, or onto your preferred makeup brush or sponge. Pro Tip: A little bit goes a long way. Start with a dime-sized amount of primer in the center of your face, and slowly work it out towards your cheeks, forehead, and chin.

If you want to apply primer to the sensitive skin around your eyelids (and keep that smoky eye looking professionally applied all day long), be sure to find a dedicated product for this area of the face. Our eyelids can collect grease throughout the day, causing a "creased" look in eyeshadow. If your eyelids are oily and you apply eyeshadow or eyeliner without primer, application may prove to be patchy and uneven.

STEP 3: LIQUID FOUNDATION

When it comes to foundation, finding the perfect shade for your skin is priority number one. The right shade of foundation can make all the difference. So how do you go about picking? Test foundation colors against your jawline. After applying, if the foundation disappears without any sort of blending, you've found your true match. This may take a bit of trial and error, but taking the time to pick the right shade is crucial.

After you've selected a product, consider the tools you'll use to apply it. Some women prefer to use their fingers, while others opt for beauty tools like brushes and sponges. If you're looking for a light coverage look, your fingers may prove to be the right applicator; however, never touch your face without thoroughly washing your hands, and be sure to wash them after application—you don't want to find your makeup handprints all over the house. For a more full-coverage look, opt for an applicator brush or beauty blender.

Start from the center of your face and blend the liquid foundation outwards. As you sweep your foundation across the skin, be sure to buff it in. Some women like to stipple a damp sponge over their foundation to help ensure it gets into those lines and creases, which can create a smoother, more even texture. Certain types of makeup brushes are also great for buffing foundation into the skin.

STEP 4: CONCEALER

There are two main categories of concealer: liquid and stick/compact.

Liquid concealer is best for the times you want light coverage over a large area of your face. Liquid concealer also works well for those looking to create a light finish, especially in areas of wrinkles, like around the eyes and mouth.

Stick and compact concealers are well-suited for heavier coverage on smaller, more specific areas of the face.

Picking the Color of Your Concealer

It's wise to invest in two shades of concealer. One should be very similar to your skin tone, and can be used to cover dark spots, pimples, and other facial blemishes. The other should be lighter than your skin tone, and can be used to highlight certain areas of the face or add clarity to your makeup look.

Note: Some women prefer to apply concealer before liquid foundation. The order of these two steps is truly a matter of preference—and trial and error. Try out both and discover which method works best for creating a smooth, radiant finish on your skin. However, when using powder foundation alone, always apply concealer first.

Where to Apply Concealer

To reduce the appearance of dark under-eye circles and create a glowing, bright look, apply light concealer beneath the eyes with a damp sponge or makeup brush.

If you're using a concealer to minimize the appearance of blemishes, apply directly to problem areas.

To highlight your face using a liquid or cream concealer, place small dots in the following areas:

Horizontally over the center of your forehead

Down the center of your nose

Under your eyes

In a curving arch at the top of your chin, just under your bottom lip

Gently blend it into the surrounding skin, and always be sure to cover with a foundation or setting powder.

How to Apply Foundation Powder

STEP 5: FOUNDATION POWDER

Applying foundation powder can be a tricky process; too little and you may as well have skipped the step altogether, too much and you'll be sporting the dreaded "cake look". In your quest for a flawless complexion, you've likely heard plenty of tricks of the trade regarding powder foundation. Keep these tips in mind to get that perfect complexion.

Using a large, fluffy powder brush, begin by dusting a light coat of powder all over your face. Press the bristles into the powder, then sweep across the skin in long, arching strokes.

If there are certain areas of your skin that need more coverage (the red and oily parts of your face are generally found in the center), you may want to apply a bit more powder. For this step, place your brush into the powder then firmly press it into the skin; this step helps the powder make its way into pores and lines for a smoother texture.

STEP 6: BRONZER

Bronzer can give your skin that sun-kissed glow all year long. Use a dedicated bronzer brush to sweep a golden tan across your face; bronzer brushes are crafted with more bristles, and placed much more tightly together, ensuring you get the most out of your colorful bronzer with each and every swipe.

How to Choose the Right Shade of Bronzer

One of the most common bronzer blunders comes in choosing the wrong shade. If you're not used to working with bronzer, use one that's two shades darker than your skin at most.

Where to Apply Bronzer

Once you've got the right shade, apply your bronzer in the shape of a number "3" on both sides of the face. Start at your forehead, pull the bronzer along your cheeks, then sweep it across the jawline, reaching all the way down to your chin. Pro Tip: Don't forget to blend it into your neck. Repeat on the opposite side.

STEP 7: BLUSH

Flushed cheeks have been a mainstay of makeup glamour for centuries. If you want to add a bit more color and vibrancy to your complexion, blush may be the key. Use a dense brush with plenty of bristles to apply your blush—this will make sure you get the most out of every blush sweep.

Where to Apply Blush

There's not a one-size-fits-all answer for blush application. Use the color of your blush to help you decide where to apply it.

Pink blush: When using pink blush, apply it only to the apples of your cheeks. Pink blush is designed to mimic the natural flush your body creates, during which blood pools into your cheeks. To find the apples of your cheeks, put on your best smile. The "apple" refers to the front part of the cheek that becomes more pronounced when you sport a grin.

Plum blush: Those with medium to dark skin tones can use plum blushes in the same way those with fair complexions use light pink blushes.

Peach blush: Instead of using pink blush on just the apples of the cheeks, utilize these shades to help sculpt your face and add just a tiny hint of color. Twist one side of your face (as if you were pursing your lips and directing them to the opposite side of the face). Then, sweep the peach blush along your cheekbones, starting near your ears and ending at the apples of your cheeks.

STEP 8: HIGHLIGHTER

The right highlighter adds a bit of glam and glow to every makeup look. Whether you're opting for a more natural look or want something bold and beautiful, highlighter can complement your makeup application.

Highlighters come in a variety of forms, including liquids, creams, and powders. You can choose to use one, or find your favorite combination of two or three. Whatever you choose, the application process remains the same.

Where to Apply Highlighter

After you've created a flawless canvas with your new foundation routine, map out the areas on your face that you wish to highlight.

Using a liquid highlighter first, apply in the following areas:

Down the bridge of your nose

Across the tops of your cheekbones

In the inner corners of your eyelids

On your brow bone

The indent above your upper lip (also called the Cupid's Bow)

The center of your forehead

The center of your chin

Once you're happy with your liquid highlighter application, blend it in using your fingertips or a sponge. To maximize the effect of your highlighting, layer in cream or powder highlighter over the areas you wish to accentuate.

Enhance your look and put your best face forward!

Colorescience has everything you need to achieve healthy, beautiful skin.

STEP 9: EYESHADOW

Eyeshadow can add interest to your makeup look, whether you opt for neutral shades or go bold with colorful hues. Whichever look you use, grab two complementary eyeshadows: one lighter shade, and one darker shade.

Dip your eyeshadow brush into the light shade, then tap the brush to get rid of any excess product. Apply the lighter shadow across the entire lid, starting at the lash line and ending just above the crease of your eyelid.

Now dip your brush into the darker color, tapping off the excess once again. Apply the color at the outer corner of your eye, just above your lash line. Sweep the darker color across your eyelid crease, just under the brow bone. Stop application around the center of your eyelid, as you don't want to darken the inner corners. Take a clean shadow brush and blend the two shades together. If you'd like a more intense look, reapply the darker shadow once more.

STEP 10: EYELINER

Applying eyeliner can be difficult—one little mistake and you're stuck with "raccoon" eyes. Banish your eye makeup woes with these essential tips for applying eyeliner.

Types of Eyeliner

Liquid eyeliner: If you're looking for precision, liquid eyeliner is your new best friend. You can find liquid liner in bottle form, which is applied with a fine dipping brush. You can also find liquid liner in a marker-type pen.

How to apply: With liquid eyeliner, start thin at the inner corner of your eye, then make the application thicker towards the outer corner. You can start lining at the middle of your eye, or in the inner corner, and keep the liner tip or brush as close to the lash line as possible. Use small strokes of your liner to create small dashes along the lash line, then connect them to fill in the gaps. If your hand slips, don't worry! Apply a bit of eye makeup remover to a Q-tip and clean up the area.

Gel eyeliner: This type of eyeliner typically comes in a small pot, with a thin brush for application. Gel eyeliner is fantastic for creating a cat-eye look.

How to apply: Dip a flat, angular brush into the gel eyeliner pot. Swirl the brush to ensure both sides have product on them, and start application in the middle of the lash line, working outwards. Then, draw a line from the inner corner of your eye towards the middle, connecting the two lines.

Pencil eyeliner: This is typically the best eyeliner option for beginners. A sharp pencil eyeliner is easy to use on your waterline, and is great for creating a smoky eye.

How to apply: Sharpen your liner pencil each time you use it. After pulling your eyelid taut, draw small light dots starting at the outer corner of your upper eyelid. Work your way into the inner corner of your eye to create a thin dotted line, as close to the lash line as possible. Connect the dots with your pencil or use a small shadow brush to blend them in.

STEP 11: MASCARA

If you're going to use only one makeup product, mascara should be at the top of your list. A few swipes of mascara can make your eyes look brighter in a single step.

You can find mascara in a variety of colors, but black and brown tend to be the most popular. Start by curling your eyelashes with an eyelash curler.

How to curl your eyelashes:

Place the curler at the base of your upper lashes, being careful not to grab any of the sensitive skin around your eyelid

Slowly close the curler

Hold it in place for a few seconds

Release gently

After your eyelashes are curled, grab your tube of mascara. Gently swirl the wand around to ensure all the bristles are coated in mascara. Pro Tip: Don't pump the wand into the tube, as this allows air to get in and may cause your mascara to clump.

Wriggle the mascara brush lightly across the roots of your lashes. This will create more volume, which you can then pull through to the ends of your lashes. If your lashes clump together, grab a clean wand and brush through them. Apply a second coat for more volume.

STEP 12: LIP GLOSS

Before applying gloss, prep your lips. If your lips are chapped and cracked, be sure to use a gentle lip scrub to remove any dead skin. Next, use a lip conditioner or moisturizer to soften the lips further. After your lip balm has absorbed, blot any excess.

Begin applying your lip gloss from the center of your lips, and drag the applicator along the length of your pout. Try to avoid pulling any gloss above your natural lip line, and smack your lips together lightly to ensure your lip gloss reaches all the nooks and crannies of your lips.

STEP 13: SETTING SPRAY & SETTING POWDER

Setting spray or setting powder can be the final touch for your makeup routine. If you want makeup that stays on all day long, without greasing, creasing, or shine, it's important to invest in a quality setting solution.

Setting sprays are designed for all skin types, and can be used to set a variety of looks, whether you're rocking light coverage or sporting a full face of beautiful makeup. Setting spray keeps your makeup in place, helping you reduce reapplication needs and keeping your makeup looking flawless for hours at a time.

Setting spray is to your face as hairspray is to your stylish do, and it's applied in a very similar fashion. Hold the bottle at least 8 inches from your face, then spritz lightly a few times to ensure all bits of your face are covered. If you want to ensure your makeup is covered from forehead to chin, first spritz in an X shape across your face, then follow it up by spraying a T shape.

There's no need to rub the spray in once applied, as it will dry naturally within seconds.

Final Look

Your makeup is complete. With these makeup applications tips, it's easy to create a variety of beauty looks, whether you're headed to the office or going out for a night on the town.

Tips for Makeup

Made in the USA
Middletown, DE
16 November 2022

15207368R00033